MEET FIREFIGHTER Jen

Elizabeth Kernan

The Rosen Publishing Group, Inc.
New York

Jen is a firefighter. Firefighters put out fires. Firefighter Jen works at a fire station.

2

Each morning, Firefighter Jen gets her boots, pants, coat, and hat ready. If the fire **alarm** rings, she can put on her **gear** quickly.

Suddenly the fire alarm rings in the fire station. Someone has called **911** to report a fire on Main Street.

Firefighter Jen puts on her gear and runs to the truck. A moment later, Jen and the other firefighters are on their way to the fire.

Firefighter Jen drives the fire truck. Firefighter Bob turns on the lights and the **siren**. The siren tells people when the fire truck is coming.

The firefighters get to the fire quickly. Firefighter Jen takes the fire **hose** off the truck.

Firefighter Jen puts out the fire with water from the hose. When the firefighters are done, they go back to the fire station.

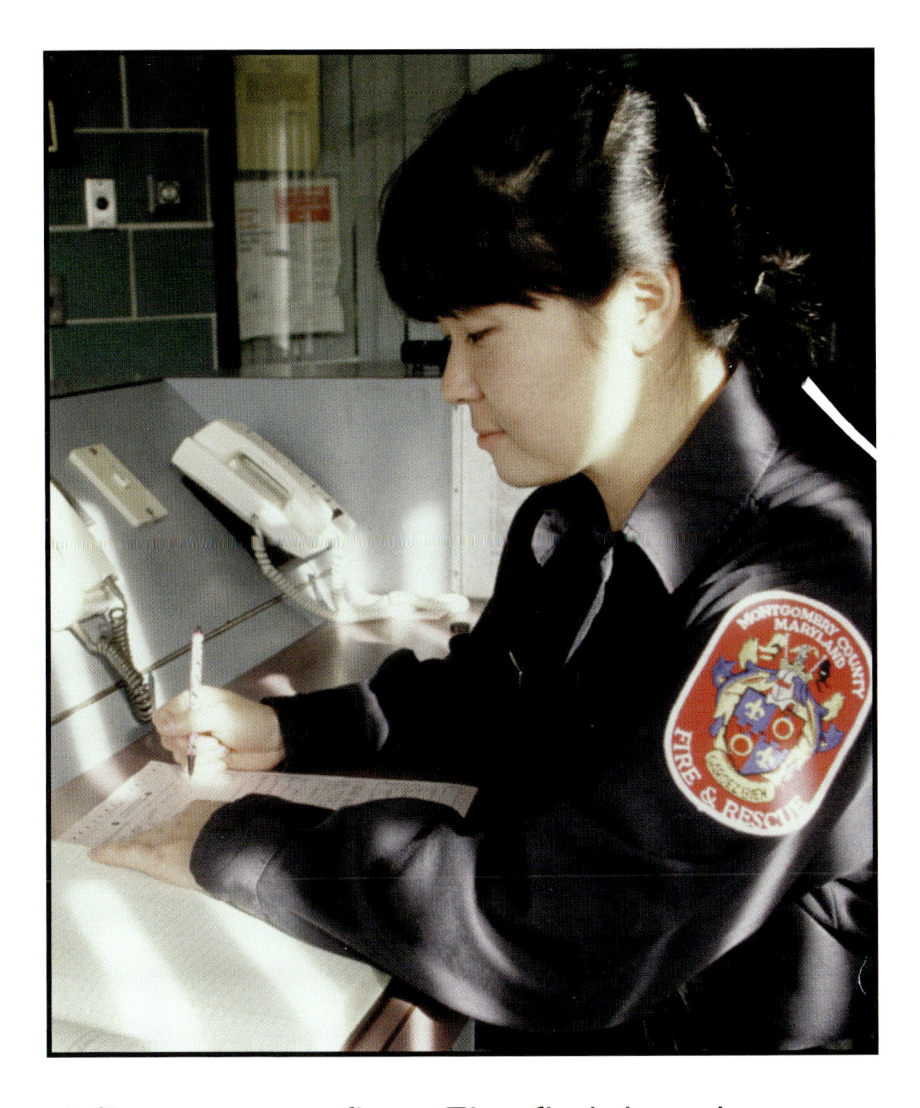

After every fire, Firefighter Jen writes a report. The report tells what the firefighters saw and did.

9

Firefighter Jen helps kids learn about **fire safety**. She also tells them what to do if their clothes catch on fire.

Firefighter Jen says, "Stop where you are. Drop to the ground. Roll around to put the fire out."

GLOSSARY

alarm — A loud bell that tells firefighters they are needed at a fire.

fire safety — Rules for what to do when a fire starts.

gear — Clothing or tools needed to do a job.

hose — A tool used to put water on a fire.

911 — The phone number that is used to reach the fire station or police station quickly.

siren — Something that makes a loud noise to let people know that the fire truck is coming.